CLOSE READING

FICTION

AGES 7+

Scholastic Education, an imprint of Scholastic Ltd
Book End, Range Road, Witney, Oxfordshire, OX29 0YD
Registered office: Westfield Road, Southam, Warwickshire CV47 0RA
www.scholastic.co.uk
© 2016, Scholastic Inc. © 2019, Scholastic Ltd
1 2 3 4 5 6 7 8 9   9 0 1 2 3 4 5 6 7 8

British Library Cataloguing-in-Publication Data
A catalogue record for this book is available from the British Library.
ISBN 978-1407-18276-6

Printed and bound by Ashford Colour Press

Author
Marcia Miller, Martin Lee
Editorial
Rachel Morgan, Louise Titley, Jane Wood and Rebecca Rothwell
Cover and Series Design
Scholastic Design Team: Nicolle Thomas, Neil Salt and Alice Duggan
Illustrations
Anne Kennedy, except page 14 by Robert W. Alley

UK Revised Edition. Originally published by Scholastic Inc, 557 Broadway, New York, NY 10012 (ISBN: 978-0-545-79385-8)

The publishers gratefully acknowledge permission to reproduce the following copyright material:
"Up the Elephant's Trunk" from *Playful Poems That Build Reading Skills* © 2000 by Kirk Mann. Used by permission of Scholastic Inc.
Every effort has been made to trace copyright holders for the works reproduced in this book, and the publishers apologise
for any inadvertent omissions.

Contents

.... Texts and Questions ....

Character

Point of View

Setting/Mood

Key Events & Details

Sequence of Events

Problem & Solution

Context Clues

Compare & Contrast

Introduction

Texts For Close Reading and Deep Comprehension

Close reading involves careful study of a short text passage to build a deep, critical understanding of the text. By developing children's comprehension and higher-order thinking skills, you can help them make sense of the world.

> "A significant body of research links the close reading of complex text – whether the student is a struggling reader or advanced – to significant gains in reading proficiency, and finds close reading to be a key component of college and career readiness."
> (Partnership for Assessment of Readiness for College and Careers, 2012, p7)

Reading and Re-Reading For Different Purposes

The texts in *Close Reading* are carefully selected and deliberately short. This focuses children on purposeful reading, re-reading and responding. They learn about the topic through rich vocabulary development and deep comprehension.

Children re-read and analyse the text through questioning to explore:

- text structure and features
- key ideas and details
- connections/conclusions
- predictions/inferences
- words and phrases in context.

Children actively respond to the text using:

- higher-order thinking skills
- paired discussion
- written responses.

Text Marking: A Powerful Active-Reading Strategy

To improve their comprehension of literary texts, children must actively engage with the material. Careful and consistent text marking by hand is one valuable way to accomplish this. The true goal of teaching text marking is to help children internalise an effective close-reading strategy, not to have them show how many marks they can make on a page. Text-marking skills are encouraged in each passage.

About the Texts and Questions

This book provides 20 reproducible texts that address eight key reading-comprehension skills:

- Character
- Point of View
- Setting/Mood
- Key Events & Details
- Sequence of Events
- Problem & Solution
- Context Clues
- Compare & Contrast

The contents pages detail the skills and genres covered as well as the Lexile score (see page 7). The passages are organised to help scaffold young children's understanding of each comprehension skill. Until your children are reading independently, the passages will work best as shared-reading activities or during guided reading so that you can scaffold and support readers. (See page 9 for a close-reading routine to model.)

Following each passage is a reproducible 'Questions' page of text-dependent comprehension questions.

Answers are provided. They include sample text marking and answers. Encourage children to self-assess and revise their answers as you review the text markings together. This approach encourages discussion, comparison, extension, reinforcement and correlation to other reading skills.

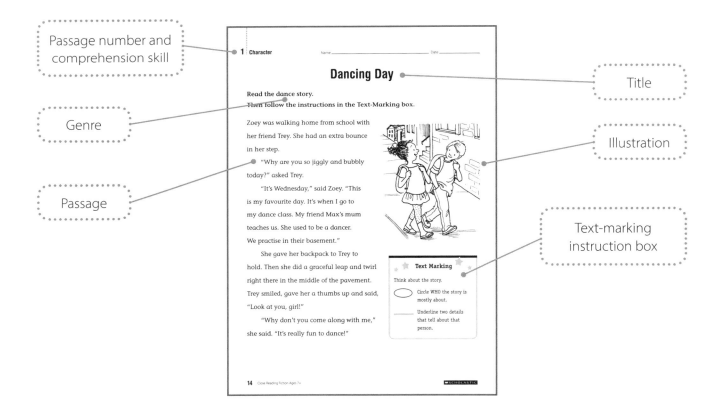

Passage number and comprehension skill

Genre

Passage

Title

Illustration

Text-marking instruction box

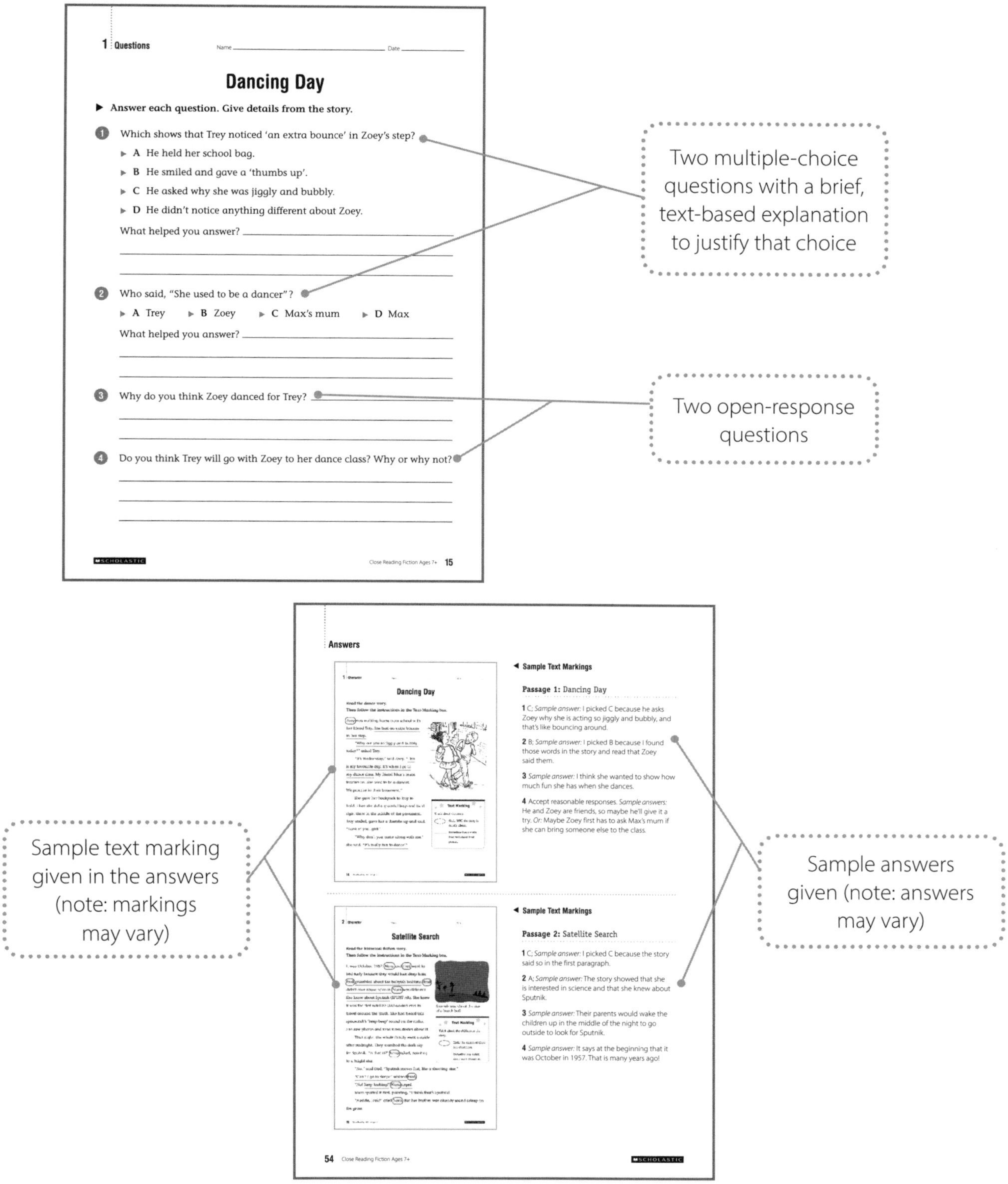
1 Questions
Name
Date
Dancing Day
Answer each question. Give details from the story.
1 Which shows that Trey noticed 'an extra bounce' in Zoey's step?
A He held her school bag.
B He smiled and gave a 'thumbs up'.
C He asked why she was jiggly and bubbly.
D He didn't notice anything different about Zoey.
What helped you answer?
2 Who said, "She used to be a dancer"?
A Trey B Zoey C Max's mum D Max
What helped you answer?
3 Why do you think Zoey danced for Trey?
4 Do you think Trey will go with Zoey to her dance class? Why or why not?
SCHOLASTIC
Close Reading Fiction Ages 7+ 15
Two multiple-choice questions with a brief, text-based explanation to justify that choice
Two open-response questions
Answers
Dancing Day
Sample Text Markings
Passage 1: Dancing Day
1 C; Sample answer: I picked C because he asks Zoey why she is acting so jiggly and bubbly, and that's like bouncing around.
2 B; Sample answer: I picked B because I found those words in the story and read that Zoey said them.
3 Sample answer: I think she wanted to show how much fun she has when she dances.
4 Accept reasonable responses. Sample answers: He and Zoey are friends, so maybe he'll give it a try. Or: Maybe Zoey first has to ask Max's mum if she can bring someone else to the class.
Satellite Search
Sample Text Markings
Passage 2: Satellite Search
1 C; Sample answer: I picked C because the story said so in the first paragraph.
2 A; Sample answer: The story showed that she is interested in science and that she knew about Sputnik.
3 Sample answer: Their parents would wake the children up in the middle of the night to go outside to look for Sputnik.
4 Sample answer: It says at the beginning that it was October in 1957. That is many years ago!
54 Close Reading Fiction Ages 7+
SCHOLASTIC
Sample text marking given in the answers (note: markings may vary)
Sample answers given (note: answers may vary)

Lexiles

The Lexile Framework® finds the right books for children by measuring readers and texts on the same scale. Lexile measures are the global standard in reading assessment and are accurate for all ages, including first- and second-language learners. The Lexile scores fall within the ranges recommended for children aged 7+. (The poem on page 22 does not include a Lexile score because poetry is excluded from Lexile measurements.)

Comprehension Skill Summary Cards

Comprehension Skill Summary Cards are provided on pages 10–13 to help support the children. The terms in bold are the same ones the children will identify as they mark the text.

Give children the relevant card before providing them with the text passage. Discuss the skill together to ensure that children understand it. Encourage the children to use the cards as a set of reading aids to refer to whenever they read any type of fiction text or display the cards in your classroom.

Tips and Suggestions

- The text-marking process is adaptable. While numbering, boxing, circling and underlining are the most common methods, you can personalise the strategy for your class. You might ask the children to use letters to mark text; for example, write 'MC' to indicate a main character, 'D' to mark a detail or 'P' for problem and 'S' for solution. Whichever technique you use, focus on the need for consistency of marking.

- You may wish to extend the text-marking strategy by asking the children to identify other aspects of writing, such as confusing words, expressions or idioms.

National Curriculum Correlation

	Passages
• listening to and discussing a wide range of fiction	1–20
• identifying themes and conventions in a wide range of books	3, 16
• checking that the text makes sense to them, discussing their understanding and explaining the meaning of words in context	4, 7, 8, 9, 10, 15, 18, 20
• drawing inferences such as inferring characters' feelings, thoughts and motives from their actions, and justifying inferences with evidence	1–20
• predicting what might happen from details stated and implied	1, 13
• identifying main ideas drawn from more than one paragraph and summarising these	9, 10, 11
• identifying how language, structure and presentation contribute to meaning	4, 5, 8, 9, 11, 19

Teaching Routine for Close Reading and Text Marking

Here is one suggested routine to use Close Reading and Text Marking in the classroom.

Preview

- **Engage prior knowledge** of passage topic and its genre. Help children link it to similar topics or examples of the genre they may have read.
- **Identify the reading skill** for which children will be marking the text. Display or distribute the relevant Comprehension Skill Summary Card and review these together. (See Comprehension Skill Summary Cards, page 8.)

Model *(for the first passage, to familiarise children with the process)*

- **Display the passage** and provide children with their own copy. Look at the text together by reading the title and looking at the illustration.
- **Draw attention to the markings** children will use to enhance their understanding of the passage. Link the text-marking box to the Comprehension Skill Summary Card for clarification.
- **Read aloud the passage** as children follow along. Guide children to think about the featured skill and to note any questions they may have on sticky notes.
- **Mark the text together.** Begin by numbering the paragraphs. Then discuss the choices you make when marking the text, demonstrating and explaining how various text elements support the skill. Check that children understand how to mark the text using the icons and graphics shown in the text-marking box.

Read

- **Display each passage for a shared reading experience.** Do a quick read of the passage together to familiarise the children with it. Then read it together a second time, pausing as necessary to answer questions, draw connections or clarify words. Then read the passage once more, this time with an eye to the features described in the text-marking box.
- **Invite children to offer ideas for additional markings.** These might include noting unfamiliar vocabulary, an idiom or phrase they may not understand, or an especially interesting, unusual or important detail they want to remember. Model how to use sticky notes, coloured pencils, highlighters or question marks.

Respond

- **If children are able, ask them to read the passage independently.** This reading is intended to allow children to mark the text themselves, with your support, as needed. It will also prepare them to discuss the passage and offer their views about it.
- **Ask the children to answer the questions on the companion questions page.** Depending on the abilities of your children, you might read aloud the questions and then have them answer orally. Model how to look back at the text markings and other text evidence for assistance. This will help children provide complete and supported responses.

Point of View

The **point of view** of a story means who is telling it.
What you learn in the story comes through that point of view.

- Some stories are told by a **narrator**. The narrator can be someone who is not in the story. Look for words like **he**, **she** and **they**.

- The narrator can be a character in the story. Look for words like **I** and **me**.

- Point of view also helps you understand how characters think and feel.

- One way to tell a character's point of view is by what he or she says.

Character

Characters are who a story is about. A character can be a person, an animal or a thing.

- Read for details that describe each character.

- Read for details that describe different characters so you can tell them apart.

- Read for details that tell if and how characters change or learn during the story.

Key Events & Details

Things happen in every story.
Events are actions or things that happen.
Events move the story along.

Some events are more important than others.

- A **key event** answers the question 'What is an important thing that happens?'

- **Details** tell more about a key event.

Setting/Mood

The **setting** of a story tells where and when the story takes place. The setting can help create the **mood** or feeling of the story.

- Read for details that tell where a story takes place.

It can be a **real** place.

It can be a **make-believe** place.

- Read for details that tell when the story takes place.

It might be set in the **present** (now).

It might be set in the **past** (long ago).

It might be set in the **future** (years from now).

- Think about how the setting helps you feel the mood of the story.

Problem & Solution

Sometimes you will read about **problems** and how they get **solved**.

- A **problem** is a kind of trouble or puzzle.
  A problem needs to be fixed or solved.

- A **solution** is how to solve a problem.
  A solution makes things better.

- **Signal words** are clues to a problem and its solutions.

Examples for problems: **question, need** and **trouble**.

Examples for solutions: **answer, idea, result, plan, reason** and **solve**.

Sequence of Events

When you read, look for the **order** in which things happen.

- **Events** are actions or things that happen in a story.

- The **sequence** is the order in which events happen.

- **Signal words** give clues about the sequence of events.

Examples: **before, first, second, next, then, now, later, after, finally** and **last**, as well as **dates** and **times**.

Compare & Contrast

Authors may describe how people, places, things or ideas are **alike** and **different**.

- To **compare** means to tell how things are the same or alike.

- To **contrast** means to tell how things are different.

- **Signal words** give clues that help you compare and contrast.

Examples for comparing: **both, too, like, also** and **in the same way.**

Examples for contrasting: **but, only, however, unlike** and **different.**

Context Clues

Authors may use words you don't know. Other words nearby may help.

- **Context** means all the words and sentences around a word you don't know.

- **Context clues** are hints that can help you work out the meaning of a word.

Look for words that mean the same or opposite.

Use details to help you understand the word.

Name _____ Date _____

Dancing Day

Read the dance story.

Then follow the instructions in the Text-Marking box.

Zoey was walking home from school with her friend Trey. She had an extra bounce in her step.

"Why are you so jiggly and bubbly today?" asked Trey.

"It's Wednesday," said Zoey. "This is my favourite day. It's when I go to my dance class. My friend Max's mum teaches us. She used to be a dancer. We practise in their basement."

She gave her backpack to Trey to hold. Then she did a graceful leap and twirl right there in the middle of the pavement. Trey smiled, gave her a thumbs up and said, "Look at you, girl!"

"Why don't you come along with me," she said. "It's really fun to dance!"

★ Text Marking ★

Think about the story.

⬭　Circle WHO the story is mostly about.

___　Underline two details that tell about that person.

Name _____ Date _____

Dancing Day

▶ **Answer each question. Give details from the story.**

1 Which shows that Trey noticed 'an extra bounce' in Zoey's step?

- ▶ **A** He held her school bag.

- ▶ **B** He smiled and gave a 'thumbs up'.

- ▶ **C** He asked why she was jiggly and bubbly.

- ▶ **D** He didn't notice anything different about Zoey.

What helped you answer? _____

_____

_____

2 Who said, "She used to be a dancer"?

- ▶ **A** Trey   ▶ **B** Zoey   ▶ **C** Max's mum   ▶ **D** Max

What helped you answer? _____

_____

_____

3 Why do you think Zoey danced for Trey? _____

_____

_____

4 Do you think Trey will go with Zoey to her dance class? Why or why not?

_____

_____

_____

Name _____ Date _____

Satellite Search

Read the historical fiction story.
Then follow the instructions in the Text-Marking box.

It was October, 1957. Nora and Fred went to bed early because they would lose sleep later. Fred grumbled about the babyish bedtime. Fred didn't care about science. Nora was different. She knew about Sputnik (*SPUHT-nik*). She knew it was the first satellite (*SAT-uh-lite*) ever to travel around the Earth. She had heard this spacecraft's 'beep-beep' sound on the radio. She saw photos and read news stories about it.

Sputnik was about the size of a beach ball.

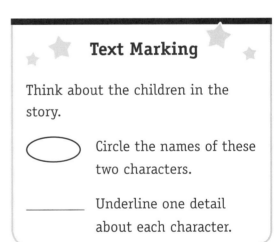

Text Marking

Think about the children in the story.

⬭ Circle the names of these two characters.

_____ Underline one detail about each character.

That night, the whole family went outside after midnight. They searched the dark sky for Sputnik. "Is that it?" Nora asked, pointing to a bright star.

"No," said Dad. "Sputnik moves fast, like a shooting star."

"Can't I go to sleep?" whined Fred.

"No! Keep looking!" Nora urged.

Mum spotted it first, pointing, "I think that's Sputnik!"

"Freddie, look!" cried Nora. But her brother was already sound asleep on the grass.

Satellite Search

▶ **Answer each question. Give details from the story.**

1 What was Sputnik?

▶ **A** a beach ball   ▶ **C** a small satellite

▶ **B** a shooting star   ▶ **D** another word for midnight

What helped you answer? _____

_____

_____

2 Which best describes Nora?

▶ **A** She is interested in science.   ▶ **C** She is a bossy person.

▶ **B** She has trouble sleeping.   ▶ **D** She has good luck.

What helped you answer? _____

_____

_____

3 Why did Nora and Fred go to sleep early that night?

_____

_____

_____

4 How do you know that this story took place in the past?

_____

_____

_____

Fox and Stork

Read the fable.

Then follow the instructions in the Text-Marking box.

One day Fox made soup. As it cooked,
Stork flew by. That gave Fox a sly idea.
He invited Stork to join him for soup.
"Come back at dark, Stork."

"How kind," Stork thought. But
Fox planned a mean trick.

Later, Fox served bowls of soup.
But Stork's bowl was too shallow for her
long beak. She could not taste one drop.
Fox slurped loudly and said, "Mmmm,
yummy!" Poor Stork felt hungry and insulted.
Still, she asked Fox to eat with her the next
night. Fox agreed.

Fox went to Stork's home for dinner.
Stork served fish stew in tall, skinny jars.
Stork's pointy beak fitted nicely, and she ate
her fill. But Fox could not taste one drop.
He went home hungry and sad.

⭐ Text Marking ⭐

Think about the fable.

(⬭) Circle the name of each character.

_____ Underline two details about each character.

Name _____ Date _____

Fox and Stork

▶ **Answer each question. Give details from the fable.**

1 What reason did Fox have to invite Stork to dinner?

   ▶ **A** He wanted to play a trick on Stork.

   ▶ **B** He had made too much soup.

   ▶ **C** He knew she was hungry.

   ▶ **D** He didn't like to eat dinner by himself.

   What helped you answer? _____

   _____

2 Which is the moral of this story?

   ▶ **A** It is not wise to be too greedy.

   ▶ **B** Birds of a feather flock together.

   ▶ **C** Whatever you do, do it with all your might.

   ▶ **D** If you play tricks on others, expect them to be played on you.

   What helped you answer? _____

   _____

3 Why couldn't Fox eat the stew Stork made?

   _____

   _____

4 Why did Fox slurp loudly and say, "Mmmm, yummy"?

   _____

   _____

Bart's Spider Scare

Read the nature story.

Then follow the instructions in the Text-Marking box.

Bart was in the garden when he spotted a scary, hairy spider. He began shouting, "A spider, a spider! Kill it quick!"

"Calm down," called Grandpa from the porch. "What's all the fuss?"

Bart told Grandpa about the spider. He led Grandpa to the garden for a look.

"Now that is a welcome sight," said Grandpa. "This spider will eat insects that could harm my plants, so I'm glad it's here." Then he said, "Welcome to my garden, spider!"

"But... I thought spiders were bad," said Bart. "Don't they bite? Don't they have poison?"

"Some spiders in other countries can hurt people, but many are helpful," said Grandpa.

"It pays to learn about nature. Then you will know which animals to stay away from. You will also know a friend when you spot one!"

Text Marking

Think about the point of view of the characters. How do they react to the spider in different ways?

☐	Draw a box around each character's name.
⬭	Circle words that the first character says.
___	Underline words that the other character says.

Bart's Spider Scare

▶ **Answer each question. Give details from the story.**

1 What word does NOT mean the same as **fuss** (paragraph 2)?

▶ **A** excitement   ▶ **B** trouble   ▶ **C** quiet   ▶ **D** worrying

What helped you answer? _____

_____

_____

2 What clues help you tell when each character is talking?

▶ **A** question marks (?)   ▶ **C** full stops (.)

▶ **B** commas (,)   ▶ **D** inverted commas (" ")

What helped you answer? _____

_____

_____

3 Why did Grandpa call the spider 'a welcome sight'?

_____

_____

4 Bart and Grandpa have different points of view about the spider. Explain how the story shows this.

_____

_____

_____

_____

Name _____ Date _____

Up the Elephant's Trunk
by Kirk Mann

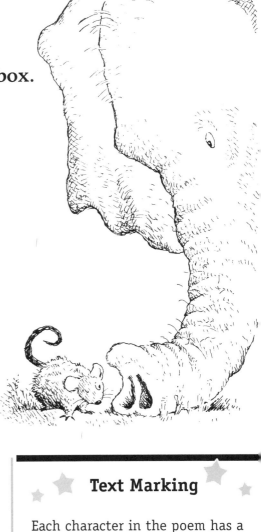

Read the poem.

Then follow the instructions in the Text-Marking box.

The elephant once said to me,

"Mouse, please climb in my nose

And go until I say to stop,

Then scratch there with your toes."

I climbed inside the long, deep trunk,

The air was damp and grey.

I walked across some peanut shells

And grass and bits of hay.

Then halfway up the bumpy trail

The elephant yelled, "Stop!"

"Scratch," he said, "with all your might,

And jump and kick and hop."

I scratched and it itched and it itched and I scratched.

He finally yelled, "Enough!"

And then he blew me out his trunk

With lots of other stuff!

⭐ Text Marking ⭐

Each character in the poem has a point of view.

☐ Draw a box around the narrator.

⬭ Circle the character that wants help.

___ Underline what the narrator does to help.

Up the Elephant's Trunk

▶ **Answer each question. Give details from the poem.**

1 What is the elephant's problem?

    ▶ **A** He is afraid of the mouse.   ▶ **C** He can't jump, kick or hop.

    ▶ **B** He has an itch he can't reach.   ▶ **D** The air in his trunk is damp.

What helped you answer? _____

_____

_____

2 Where is the mouse for most of the poem?

    ▶ **A** on the elephant's trunk   ▶ **C** far from the elephant's trunk

    ▶ **B** on a path beside the elephant   ▶ **D** inside the elephant's trunk

What helped you answer? _____

_____

_____

3 What does 'the bumpy trail' describe?

_____

_____

4 Think about the mouse. What can you say about its character?

_____

_____

_____

_____

Name _____   Date _____

Waterfall of Light

Read the holiday story.

Then follow the instructions in the Text-Marking box.

Shun Park was crowded with excited people. They stood in groups or sat on folding chairs or benches. The cold night sky was filled with stars. Soon it would be filled with brighter, more colourful stars – Chinese New Year fireworks. I could hardly wait!

"Have some noodles, Ming," my dad said. But I was too excited to eat. Then the fireworks started.

First came a loud 'BOOM', then a whistling noise. Red, orange and gold fireworks lit up the night. Sparks showered down. They looked like a waterfall of light. Everyone gazed up at the sky. People clapped and cried "Oooh!" and "Ahhh!" Then, with one last 'BOOM!' three, four, five fireworks went up at once. The sky exploded with colour. Happy New Year!

Text Marking

Think about the setting and mood of the story.

▭	Draw a box around WHEN the story takes place.
⬭	Circle WHERE the story takes place.
_____	Underline two details that set the mood.

Waterfall of Light

▶ **Answer each question. Give details from the story.**

1 Where does the story take place?

    ▶ **A** in a park   ▶ **C** at a waterfall

    ▶ **B** in the night   ▶ **D** on a folding chair

What helped you answer? _____

_____

_____

2 Why didn't Ming want to eat?

    ▶ **A** It was too cold.   ▶ **C** She didn't like noodles.

    ▶ **B** She was too excited.   ▶ **D** She was too sleepy.

What helped you answer? _____

_____

3 Why did people clap and shout that night?

_____

_____

_____

4 Explain the title of this story. _____

_____

_____

_____

_____

Name _____ Date _____

The Orphan Train

Read the historical fiction story.

Then follow the instructions in the Text-Marking box.

Hannah stared out the window of a train heading west. She saw no houses, just endless flat land. The prairie seemed like a lonely place. Hannah felt weary. The eight-year-old had bounced on her hard train seat for three days.

Only days ago, Hannah was a homeless orphan living on the streets of New York City. She was rescued by people at the Children's Aid Society (*suh-SYE-uh-tee*). They put her on a train to go and live with a farm family in Kansas. "They have room for you," she was told. In 1854, a child like her without parents was lucky to find a home anywhere. Hannah's future lay ahead, but she knew nothing of Kansas or farming. What if she didn't like the family? What if they disliked her?

Text Marking

Think about the setting and mood of the story.

☐ Draw a box around WHEN the story takes place.

⬭ Circle WHERE the story takes place.

_____ Underline two details that set the mood.

The Orphan Train

▶ **Answer each question. Give details from the story.**

1 What does the word **orphan** mean (paragraph 2)?

▶ **A** a child who does not have parents   ▶ **C** a farmer

▶ **B** a lost pet   ▶ **D** a homeless person

What helped you answer? _____

_____

2 How do you think Hannah felt during the train ride?

▶ **A** hungry   ▶ **B** happy   ▶ **C** excited   ▶ **D** worried

What helped you answer? _____

_____

_____

3 What do you think a **prairie** is (paragraph 1)? _____

_____

_____

4 How does the setting of the story help set the mood?
Use another sheet of paper for your answer.

Name _____ Date _____

Picnic for Three

Read the holiday story.

Then follow the instructions in the Text-Marking box.

Sasha, her dog, Petey, and her older cousin Mikel were in a rowing boat one August afternoon. Mikel was rowing them to a nearby island for a picnic. It was a short boat ride away. A light breeze blew and the sun was shining. The waves lapped gently against the boat.

Suddenly, the sun disappeared behind dark clouds and everything changed. The gentle breeze became a wild wind that blew Sasha's hair and whipped at her clothes. The water became choppy and rocked the small boat from side to side. Then it began to pour.

"We must get back to shore," Mikel yelled. He rowed as hard as he could to reach safety. Petey barked and shook, so Sasha held him close. With her free hand, she gripped her seat tightly. The picnic would have to wait.

Text Marking

Think about the setting and mood of the story.

☐ Draw a box around WHEN the story takes place.

◯ Circle WHERE the story takes place.

_____ Underline three details that set the mood.

Picnic for Three

▶ **Answer each question. Give details from the story.**

1 When does the story take place?

- ▶ **A** during the night
- ▶ **C** in the morning
- ▶ **B** during the afternoon
- ▶ **D** at lunch time

What helped you answer? _____

_____

2 What is the main reason the mood of the story changes?

- ▶ **A** Rain began to pour down.
- ▶ **B** Petey started barking.
- ▶ **C** Sasha and Mikel got too hungry to wait.
- ▶ **D** The weather went from calm to stormy.

What helped you answer? _____

_____

_____

_____

3 Describe what this sentence from the story means:
'The waves lapped gently against the boat.'

_____

_____

_____

4 Explain the last sentence of the story. Use another sheet of paper.

Rusty Stones

Read the science-fiction story.

Then follow the instructions in the Text-Marking box.

Willa couldn't believe her eyes. There was a giant hole on her farm. Only the night before, tall corn had grown there. "What happened?" wondered Willa. She got off her tractor to explore the hole. Willa walked all the way around it. She saw packed dirt and rust-coloured blobs of stone.

Slowly, Willa stepped into the strange hole to grab a small stone. How heavy and warm it felt! Suddenly, the stone began to jiggle in her hand. A squeaky voice cried, "KLEEP!" Willa looked more closely. She saw a crack that was bright purple inside. She noticed that the other rusty stones had the same look. They were also jiggling.

"What?" Willa thought. "Did a fleet of tiny spaceships crash into my farm?"

Text Marking

Think about the events in the story.

( )   Circle two key events that happen.

_____   Underline one detail about each event.

Rusty Stones

▶ **Answer each question. Give details from the story.**

1 What surprised Willa first about the rusty stones?

▶ **A** They could speak.   ▶ **C** They looked like spaceships.

▶ **B** They were heavy and warm.   ▶ **D** They covered her cornfield.

What helped you answer? _____

_____

_____

2 What did Willa think had happened at her farm?

▶ **A** Tiny spaceships had landed.   ▶ **C** The corn turned purple.

▶ **B** There was a bad storm.   ▶ **D** Her tractor broke down.

What helped you answer? _____

_____

3 Look at the picture. Which part of the story does it show? Explain.

_____

_____

_____

_____

4 A voice cried, "KLEEP!" What might that word mean? Explain your idea.

_____

_____

_____

Where's Frankie?

Read the mystery story.
Then follow the instructions in the Text-Marking box.

A funny thing happened one day when Ike went to feed Frankie. He was not in his tank or near it. Where had Ike's frog disappeared to?

Ike put down the frog food to search for his missing pet. He looked in the kitchen and behind the sofa in the living room. He searched under the beds in the bedrooms. He even opened all the cupboard doors and peeked in. No luck. Frankie was missing, and Ike was in tears.

"Now, THINK," Ike told himself, "What do frogs like? Where might Frankie want to be?" The lightbulb in Ike's head lit up brightly. He raced to the bathroom with a happy and knowing smile. There was Frankie in the bath by the plughole. He seemed to be smiling, too.

★ ★ Text Marking ★ ★

Think about the events in the story.

⬭ Circle two key events that happen.

_____ Underline one detail about each event.

Name _____ Date _____

Where's Frankie?

▶ **Answer each question. Give details from the mystery.**

1 Why did Ike cry?

▶ **A** Frankie was hungry. ▶ **C** Frankie was lost.

▶ **B** Ike was hungry. ▶ **D** Ike was lost.

What helped you answer? _____

_____

2 What does 'The lightbulb in his head lit up brightly' mean?

▶ **A** Ike got a headache. ▶ **C** Ike smiled from ear to ear.

▶ **B** Ike got a clever idea. ▶ **D** Ike looked too long at the lamp.

What helped you answer? _____

_____

_____

3 What helped Ike work out where to find Frankie?

_____

_____

_____

4 Retell the main events of the story in a few sentences.

_____

_____

_____

_____

Name _____   Date _____

Seeing the Seaport

Read the travel story.

Then follow the instructions in the Text-Marking box.

The Loh family entered the visitor centre of the old seaport. There they planned their day. They picked out which activities, displays and shows to see. They took a map of the seaport and began their tour.

First, the Lohs strolled all around the seaport. It looked as it did when it was filled with sailors, ship builders and workers. Guides dressed the way people did 150 years ago. They told sailing stories. They sang sea songs. They worked on their crafts as visitors watched.

Next, the Lohs boarded three old sailing ships. Macey especially liked the wooden whale boat. Devin liked the old-fashioned fire boat. Mr Loh said that visiting old ships can turn *landlubbers* into *sea dogs*.

Text Marking

Think about the events in the story.

⬭ Circle three key events on the Loh family's tour.

_____ Underline one detail about each event.

Name _____ Date _____

Seeing the Seaport

► **Answer each question. Give details from the story.**

1 What did the Loh family do at the visitor centre?

   ► **A** They sang whaling songs. ► **C** They visited an old fire boat.

   ► **B** They turned into sea dogs. ► **D** They decided which things to see.

What helped you answer? _____

_____

2 Who would rather NOT go to sea?

   ► **A** sea dogs   ► **B** landlubbers   ► **C** sailors   ► **D** guides

What helped you answer? _____

_____

_____

_____

3 Look at the picture. How does it help you understand the story?

_____

_____

_____

4 Re-read the last sentence of the story. What did Mr Loh mean?

_____

_____

_____

A New Sitter

Read the realistic fiction story.
Then follow the instructions in the Text-Marking box.

Roxy rang the doorbell at 6pm. She
was the new babysitter. Tia frowned
when Dad introduced them. "Where's
Pam?" Tia grumbled. Pam was her
usual sitter. Tia slumped onto the
sofa. She folded her arms across her
chest and began to sulk.

After Tia's dad left, Roxy knew
just what to do. She suggested
making puppets together. Tia's frown
turned into a smile. Tia and Roxy made
paper-bag puppets. They used them to
put on a silly play. The girls laughed and
giggled all evening.

Tia's dad returned just before bedtime.
"Dad, can Roxy be my sitter next time?"
Tia asked. "She's the best!"

Text Marking

Find the sequence of events for
Tia's evening.

☐	Draw boxes around the signal words: **at 6pm**, **after** and **before bedtime**.
___	Underline three important events.
1–2–3	Number the events in order.

A New Sitter

▶ **Answer each question. Give details from the story.**

1 Who was Pam?

  ▶ **A** the new babysitter   ▶ **C** the father

  ▶ **B** the old babysitter   ▶ **D** the child

What helped you answer? _____

_____

2 What happened in the middle of the story?

  ▶ **A** Roxy arrived at Tia's house.   ▶ **C** Tia and Roxy made puppets.

  ▶ **B** Tia sulked on the sofa.   ▶ **D** Dad got home.

What helped you answer? _____

_____

_____

3 What made Tia change her mind about Roxy? Explain.

_____

_____

_____

4 What can you learn from this story about meeting new people?

_____

_____

_____

_____

Name _____ Date _____

Friends Play Putt-Putt

Read the sports story.

Then follow the instructions in the Text-Marking box.

Mum took Kai and Emily to Putt-Putt to play mini-golf. The first thing they did was to choose their golf equipment. Each picked a putter and a ball. Emily chose a yellow ball and Kai took a blue one.

Next, they walked to the golf course and looked it over.

Then, Emily and Kai played the first hole. It was called Windmill. Kai went first and hit the ball with his putter. The ball hit the moving windmill and bounced back to him. Both children laughed. Kai's second putt was better. He and Emily both got their balls into the hole in five goes. Emily kept track of their scores.

After they finished playing Windmill, the friends walked to the second hole. It was called Bridge. Emily went first this time. She aimed carefully at the narrow bridge...

Text Marking

Find the sequence of events at Putt-Putt.

☐	Draw boxes around the signal words: **first**, **next**, **then** and **after**.
‎_____	Underline the most important events.
1–2–3–4	Number the events in order.

Friends Play Putt-Putt

▶ **Answer each question. Give details from the story.**

1 Which piece of **equipment** did Kai and Emily pick (paragraph 1)?

▶ **A** a windmill   ▶ **B** a bridge   ▶ **C** a putter   ▶ **D** a hole

What helped you answer? _____

_____

2 When you 'play a hole' in mini-golf, you _____.

▶ **A** putt the ball until you get it in the hole

▶ **B** putt the ball around the hole so it never falls in

▶ **C** play music as you walk the holes in the golf course

▶ **D** pretend to fall down and use the putter to get up

What helped you answer? _____

_____

3 Describe what Kai and Emily did BEFORE they played the Windmill hole.

_____

_____

_____

4 Predict: What do you think might happen when Emily plays the Bridge?

_____

_____

_____

_____

Name _____ Date _____

Family Fun

Read the adventure story.

Then follow the instructions in the Text-Marking box.

The Perez family arrived at FunLand at 10am sharp. Mum paid the entrance fee and picked up tickets for the rides. Excitement lay ahead!

After they skipped through the gates, they looked for the first ride to try. The colourful spinning teacups grabbed their attention. All four of them fitted into one giant cup. "That was great!" Alonzo laughed. But the spinning made Luisa dizzy.

Next, they went to the bumper cars. Mum and Alonzo happily crashed about on this bumpy ride. Luisa and Dad watched and took photos. Luisa began to feel better.

Finally, they all rode on the scary rollercoaster. Mum screamed the whole time and Dad looked like a stone statue. But Alonzo and Luisa loved every speedy minute!

Text Marking

Find the sequence of events at FunLand.

☐	Draw boxes around the signal words and times.
___	Underline the most important events.
1–2–3–4	Number the events in order.

Name _____ Date _____

Family Fun

▶ **Answer each question. Give details from the adventure.**

1 What was the third ride the Perez family went on?

▶ **A** the rollercoaster   ▶ **C** the entrance gate

▶ **B** the spinning teacups   ▶ **D** the bumper cars

What helped you answer? _____

_____

2 Why did Luisa watch with Dad at the bumper cars?

▶ **A** Luisa was scared of that ride.

▶ **B** Dad was too big for that ride.

▶ **C** She and Dad wanted something to eat.

▶ **D** Luisa was dizzy from the first ride.

What helped you answer? _____

_____

_____

3 How did the Perez family show that they knew 'Excitement lay ahead'?

_____

_____

4 How did each member of the family react to the rollercoaster ride?

_____

_____

_____

Name _____   Date _____

Fishing for the Moon

Read the Chinese folktale.

Then follow the instructions in the Text-Marking box.

One clear night, Quan went to fetch water. He got a big surprise when he reached the village well. Deep down in the water was the moon. Its silvery face looked up at Quan.

"What a problem! Poor moon is stuck!" cried Quan as he raced home for his largest hook. He tied it to his bucket. Back at the well, he lowered the bucket to fish out the moon.

He jiggled the hook until he felt it catch. How he pulled and tugged! He yanked so hard that the rope on the bucket broke. Quan fell flat on his back. But when he looked up, the moon was back up high in the sky! Quan puffed up with pride. His plan had worked. He was the hero who rescued the moon.

Text Marking

Find the problem and Quan's solution.

☐   Draw boxes around the signal words: **problem**, **plan** and **rescued**.

◯   Circle the problem.

____   Underline Quan's solution.

Fishing for the Moon

▶ **Answer each question. Give details from the folktale.**

1 What surprise did Quan get at the village well?

  ▶ **A** He lost his hook.   ▶ **C** There was no more water.

  ▶ **B** There was no bucket.   ▶ **D** The moon was stuck in the well.

What helped you answer? _____

_____

2 Which word means the same as **rescued** (paragraph 3)?

  ▶ **A** saved   ▶ **B** raced   ▶ **C** puffed up   ▶ **D** tugged

What helped you answer? _____

_____

_____

_____

3 Why did Quan go to the village that night?

_____

_____

4 Do you think Quan was a real hero? Explain.

_____

_____

_____

_____

_____

Name _____   Date _____

Bear Tale

Read the tall tale.

Then follow the instructions in the Text-Marking box.

Uncle Jake likes to tell a tale of trouble he found while exploring a cave in the woods. The problem was that he surprised a bear named Grizz. Grizz stood up tall and let out a mighty roar.

The first thought Uncle Jake had was to run. He ran as fast as he could. But Grizz ran after him and was catching up. Then Uncle Jake had a clever idea – he dropped his camera. That stopped Grizz in his tracks. Grizz grabbed the camera, took a selfie and rolled over laughing.

Grizz called Uncle Jake over to show him the photo. Uncle Jake laughed, too. That's how man and bear became friends. Whenever Uncle Jake is in those woods, he finds Grizz. They take pictures until they fall down giggling.

Text Marking

Find the problem and the solutions.

☐ Draw boxes around the signal words: **trouble**, **problem**, **first thought** and **clever idea**.

⬭ Circle the problem.

___ Underline two solutions.

Bear Tale

▶ **Answer each question. Give details from the tall tale.**

1 Where did Uncle Jake first come across Grizz?

▶ **A** in a zoo   ▶ **B** in a cave   ▶ **C** at a circus   ▶ **D** in his garden

What helped you answer? _____

_____

2 What was the first solution Uncle Jake tried?

▶ **A** He ran.   ▶ **C** He called for help.

▶ **B** He stood up tall.   ▶ **D** He gave a mighty roar.

What helped you answer? _____

_____

3 Why did Uncle Jake need a better solution? Explain.

_____

_____

_____

_____

4 Describe two or more clues that help you know this story is a tall tale.

_____

_____

_____

_____

_____

Name _____ Date _____

Ozzie's Goal

Read the circus story.

Then follow the instructions in the Text-Marking box.

Ozzie's dad performed in the circus. He did tricks on the high wire. He danced, walked backwards and spun around up there and made it look easy! Ozzie admired his dad; he was his hero. But Ozzie didn't want to be exactly like him.

Ozzie's dream was to juggle. He set his heart on it. Dee-Dee the Clown helped by giving him beanbags to work with. Beanbags don't break or roll away when they drop. Dee-Dee used them to learn juggling herself. It was hard for Ozzie at first. But he practised every day. Ozzie wanted to learn to juggle very much.

After a month, Ozzie was juggling beanbags easily. "Soon you'll be juggling eggs!" Dee-Dee said with a wink. That did it – Ozzie had his next goal. He would get good enough to juggle raw eggs!

Text Marking

Use context clues to unlock the meaning of words.

◯ Circle the word: **admired** and the sentence: **He set his heart on it**.

_____ Underline context clues for each.

Name _____ Date _____

Ozzie's Goal

▶ **Answer each question. Give details from the story.**

1 Another way to say **admired** (paragraph 1) is _____.

▶ **A** practised   ▶ **B** looked up to   ▶ **C** got better   ▶ **D** feared

What helped you answer? _____

_____

2 Why did Ozzie practise juggling every day?

▶ **A** He wanted to make his dad proud of him.

▶ **B** He wanted to be a clown.

▶ **C** He wanted to become a good juggler.

▶ **D** It was the only thing he cared about.

What helped you answer? _____

_____

3 What do you do when you 'set your heart on' something? Explain.

_____

_____

_____

4 Why did Dee-Dee the Clown wink when she spoke about juggling eggs?

_____

_____

_____

Name _____ Date _____

Holding Hands

Read the family story.

Then follow the instructions in the Text-Marking box.

Ellie, Dad and her little brother Luke
drove to the shopping centre. Twelve-
year-old Ellie sat in the back seat,
safely wearing her seatbelt. But Luke
was just two years old. He was tucked
into his car seat beside her. Ellie kept
turning her head around like an owl.
She played 'Peek-a-Boo' with Luke to
hear his happy giggle.

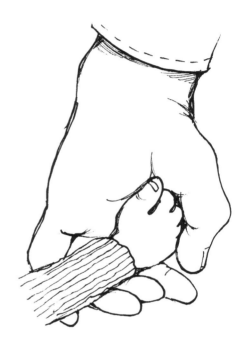

After getting out of the car, Dad
clutched Luke's right hand. The three walked
towards the shopping centre together. Luke's
tiny hand disappeared into Dad's immense
one. Ellie knew that Luke felt protected. Ellie
remembered that secure feeling herself. She
also used to hold her father's huge hand
when she was learning to walk. She always
knew Dad would keep her safe. She knew that Luke would be safe, too.

Text Marking

Use context clues to unlock the
meanings of words.

◯   Circle the words:
        clutched and **immense**.

_____   Underline context clues
        for each word.

Name _____ Date _____

Holding Hands

▶ **Answer each question. Give details from the story.**

1 Another word for **clutched** (paragraph 2) is _____.

   ▶ **A** wrapped   ▶ **B** washed   ▶ **C** rubbed   ▶ **D** held

What helped you answer? _____

_____

_____

2 What memory came to Ellie that day?

   ▶ **A** She remembered riding in a car seat.

   ▶ **B** She remembered learning to walk.

   ▶ **C** She remembered going to the shopping centre.

   ▶ **D** She remembered what to buy at the shopping centre.

What helped you answer? _____

_____

3 How does Ellie feel about her brother Luke? Explain.

_____

_____

_____

4 Look at the picture. How does it help you know the meaning of **immense** (paragraph 2)?

_____

_____

_____

Name _____   Date _____

A Pair of Pots

Read the art story.

Then follow the instructions in the Text-Marking box.

Lamar loved working with clay. He took a pottery class. The last class was a pottery party. The students took turns describing two different pots they made. Lamar talked about his coil pot and his slab pot.

"For both pots, I used red clay that dries hard," said Lamar. "I used only my hands to make the coil pot. First I made a long clay snake. Then I coiled it around and around into a pot. I smoothed the inside to finish it.

"But for the slab pot, I used tools and my hands. I used a rolling pin to flatten the clay. I used a knife to cut five squares. I pieced them together into a pot. Then I smoothed all the seams."

Text Marking

Compare and contrast making coil pots and slab pots.

☐ Draw boxes around the signal words: **both, only** and **but**.

⬭ Circle one way they are alike.

___ Underline one way they are different.

A Pair of Pots

▶ **Answer each question. Give details from the story.**

1 How were Lamar's coil pot and slab pot alike?

> ▶ **A** Both were made of stone.   ▶ **C** Both were made at pottery class.

> ▶ **B** Both were made with tools.   ▶ **D** Both were made only by hand.

What helped you answer? _____

_____

2 What did Lamar do FIRST to make his slab pot?

> ▶ **A** He flattened out the clay.   ▶ **C** He smoothed out the seams.

> ▶ **B** He cut the clay into squares.   ▶ **D** He let the pot dry.

What helped you answer? _____

_____

3 Explain the main way that making coil pots is different from making slab pots.

_____

_____

_____

_____

4 Look at the picture. Use what Lamar said to tell what it shows.

_____

_____

_____

Name _____ Date _____

Spring Play

Read the theatre story.

Then follow the instructions in the Text-Marking box.

Nikki, Meg and Hari took part in the spring play at Pine Forest School. It was a musical set in a kingdom from long ago. Meg and Hari acted in the play. But Nikki took part in a different way. She was the director. She helped the actors do their best. Nikki told them where to stand, how to speak and sing, and how to move around the stage.

Meg starred as the king. She got to wear a shiny gold crown and a long purple robe. By contrast, Hari played a jester. He wore a pointy hat with bells. Nikki taught him a funny dance, which he learned quickly and well.

The play was a hit. The whole audience cheered at the end, so Meg, Hari, Nikki and the others took five bows!

Text Marking

Compare and contrast what Nikki, Meg and Hari did in the story.

| | Draw boxes around the signal words: **but**, **different** and **by contrast**. |

Circle two things they did that was the same.

_____ Underline things they did that were different.

Name _____ Date _____

Spring Play

▶ **Answer each question. Give details from the story.**

1 What is the job of a play's **director** (paragraph 1)?

  ▶ **A** to act in the play

  ▶ **B** to help the actors play their parts

  ▶ **C** to sing and dance

  ▶ **D** to sell tickets and hand out programmes

  What helped you answer? _____

  _____

2 Who danced in the spring play?

  ▶ **A** Pine Forest School   ▶ **B** Meg   ▶ **C** Nikki   ▶ **D** Hari

  What helped you answer? _____

  _____

3 What does it mean that the play was a **hit** (paragraph 3)?

  _____

  _____

  _____

4 How were Meg and Hari's parts in the play alike?
  How were they different?

  _____

  _____

  _____

  _____

Answers

1 Character   Name _____   Date _____

Dancing Day

Read the dance story.
Then follow the instructions in the Text-Marking box.

(Zoey) was walking home from school with her friend Trey. She had an extra bounce in her step.

"Why are you so jiggly and bubbly today?" asked Trey.

"It's Wednesday," said Zoey. "This is my favourite day. It's when I go to my dance class. My friend Max's mum teaches us. She used to be a dancer. We practise in their basement."

She gave her backpack to Trey to hold. Then she did a graceful leap and twirl right there in the middle of the pavement. Trey smiled, gave her a thumbs up and said, "Look at you, girl!"

"Why don't you come along with me," she said. "It's really fun to dance!"

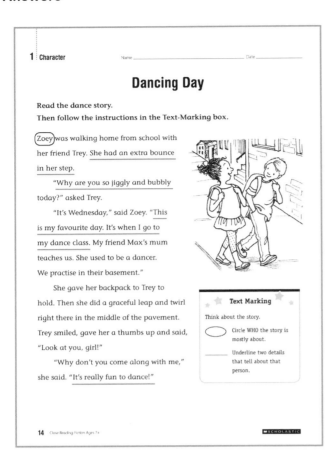

> ★ ★ **Text Marking** ★ ★
>
> Think about the story.
>
> ⬭ Circle WHO the story is mostly about.
>
> ___ Underline two details that tell about that person.

■ SCHOLASTIC

◀ **Sample Text Markings**

Passage 1: Dancing Day

1 C; *Sample answer:* I picked C because he asks Zoey why she is acting so jiggly and bubbly, and that's like bouncing around.

2 B; *Sample answer:* I picked B because I found those words in the story and read that Zoey said them.

3 *Sample answer:* I think she wanted to show how much fun she has when she dances.

4 Accept reasonable responses. *Sample answers:* He and Zoey are friends, so maybe he'll give it a try. *Or:* Maybe Zoey first has to ask Max's mum if she can bring someone else to the class.

---

2 Character   Name _____   Date _____

Satellite Search

Read the historical fiction story.
Then follow the instructions in the Text-Marking box.

It was October, 1957. (Nora) and (Fred) went to bed early because they would lose sleep later. (Fred) grumbled about the babyish bedtime. (Fred) didn't care about science. (Nora) was different. She knew about Sputnik (*SPUHT-nik*). She knew it was the first satellite (*SAT-uh-lite*) ever to travel around the Earth. She had heard this spacecraft's 'beep-beep' sound on the radio. She saw photos and read news stories about it.

That night, the whole family went outside after midnight. They searched the dark sky for Sputnik. "Is that it?" (Nora) asked, pointing to a bright star.

"No," said Dad. "Sputnik moves fast, like a shooting star."

"Can't I go to sleep?" whined (Fred)

"No! Keep looking!" (Nora) urged.

Mum spotted it first, pointing, "I think that's Sputnik!"

"Freddie, look!" cried (Nora) But her brother was already sound asleep on the grass.

Sputnik was about the size of a beach ball.

> ★ ★ **Text Marking** ★ ★
>
> Think about the children in the story.
>
> ⬭ Circle the names of these two characters.
>
> ___ Underline one detail about each character.

■ SCHOLASTIC

◀ **Sample Text Markings**

Passage 2: Satellite Search

1 C; *Sample answer:* I picked C because the story said so in the first paragraph.

2 A; *Sample answer:* The story showed that she is interested in science and that she knew about Sputnik.

3 *Sample answer:* Their parents would wake the children up in the middle of the night to go outside to look for Sputnik.

4 *Sample answer:* It says at the beginning that it was October in 1957. That is many years ago!

■ SCHOLASTIC

3 | Character
Name _____ Date _____

Fox and Stork

Read the fable.
Then follow the instructions in the Text-Marking box.

One day (Fox) made soup. As it cooked, (Stork) flew by. That gave Fox a sly idea. He invited Stork to join him for soup. "Come back at dark, Stork."

"How kind," Stork thought. But Fox planned a mean trick.

Later, Fox served bowls of soup. But Stork's bowl was too shallow for her long beak. She could not taste one drop. Fox slurped loudly and said, "Mmmm, yummy!" Poor Stork felt hungry and insulted. Still, she asked Fox to eat with her the next night. Fox agreed.

Fox went to Stork's home for dinner. Stork served fish stew in tall, skinny jars. Stork's pointy beak fitted nicely, and she ate her fill. But Fox could not taste one drop. He went home hungry and sad.

> ★ **Text Marking** ★
> Think about the fable.
> ⬭ Circle the name of each character.
> ___ Underline two details about each character.

18 Close Reading Fiction Ages 7+   ■SCHOLASTIC

---

4 | Point of View
Name _____ Date _____

Bart's Spider Scare

Read the nature story.
Then follow the instructions in the Text-Marking box.

Bart was in the garden when he spotted a scary, hairy spider. He began shouting, "A spider, a spider! Kill it quick!"

"Calm down," called Grandpa from the porch. "What's all the fuss?"

Bart told Grandpa about the spider. He led Grandpa to the garden for a look.

"Now that is a welcome sight," said Grandpa. "This spider will eat insects that could harm my plants, so I'm glad it's here." Then he said, "Welcome to my garden, spider!"

"But… I thought spiders were bad," said Bart. "Don't they bite? Don't they have poison?"

"Some spiders in other countries can hurt people, but many are helpful," said Grandpa. "It pays to learn about nature. Then you will know which animals to stay away from. You will also know a friend when you spot one!"

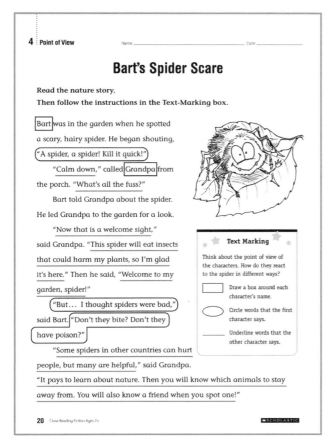

> ★ **Text Marking** ★
> Think about the point of view of the characters. How do they react to the spider in different ways?
> ☐ Draw a box around each character's name.
> ⬭ Circle words that the first character says.
> ___ Underline words that the other character says.

20 Close Reading Fiction Ages 7+   ■SCHOLASTIC

◀ **Sample Text Markings**

Passage 3: Fox and Stork

1 A; *Sample answer:* I picked A because the story said so in the first paragraph.

2 D; *Sample answer:* In this story, the fox tricked the stork about dinner and she tricked him the next night in the same way.

3 *Sample answer:* He didn't have a long beak that could fit into the tall, skinny jar she served it in.

4 *Sample answer:* I think he did that to make fun of Stork having trouble eating from the shallow bowl.

◀ **Sample Text Markings**

Passage 4: Bart's Spider Scare

1 C; *Sample answer:* I picked C because Bart wasn't quiet at all when he was shouting about the spider.

2 D; *Sample answer:* I picked D because those marks are used to show words a character says.

3 *Sample answer:* Grandpa wasn't afraid of the spider. He knew it would be helpful to his garden.

4 *Sample answer:* Bart shouts that he wants the spider dead because he is afraid of it and thinks spiders are bad. But Grandpa knows that spiders are good for his garden and is happy to see the spider.

Answers

◀ **Sample Text Markings**

Passage 5: Up the Elephant's Trunk

1 B; *Sample answer:* I picked B because that's why he asks the mouse for help.

2 D; *Sample answer:* The poem made me picture the mouse climbing inside the long, deep trunk and described what he did in there.

3 *Sample answer:* It describes the inside of the elephant's long trunk.

4 *Sample answer:* The mouse is kind and helpful, and doesn't complain. He does what the elephant asks.

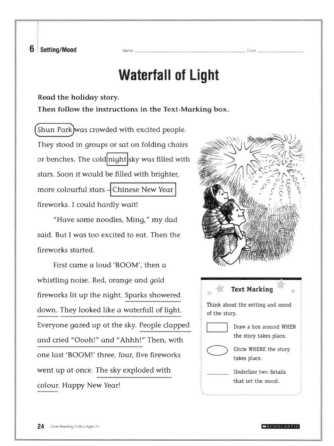

◀ **Sample Text Markings**

Passage 6: Waterfall of Light

1 A; *Sample answer:* I picked A because the story says, 'Shun Park was crowded with excited people'.

2 B; *Sample answer:* I picked B because it said that in the middle of the story.

3 *Sample answer:* I think they really enjoyed the fireworks show.

4 *Sample answer:* When the fireworks exploded, bright colourful sparks of light fell down from the sky. They kept coming down, like the water in a waterfall.

■SCHOLASTIC

The Orphan Train

Read the historical fiction story.
Then follow the instructions in the Text-Marking box.

Hannah stared out the window of a train heading west. She saw no houses, just endless flat land. The prairie seemed like a lonely place. Hannah felt weary. The eight-year-old had bounced on her hard train seat for three days.

Only days ago, Hannah was a homeless orphan living on the streets of New York City. She was rescued by people at the Children's Aid Society (*suh-SYE-uh-tee*). They put her on a train to go and live with a farm family in Kansas. "They have room for you," she was told. In 1854, a child like her without parents was lucky to find a home anywhere. Hannah's future lay ahead, but she knew nothing of Kansas or farming. What if she didn't like the family? What if they disliked her?

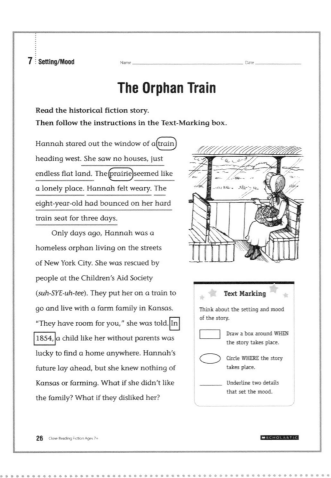

Text Marking

Think about the setting and mood of the story.

☐ Draw a box around WHEN the story takes place.

◯ Circle WHERE the story takes place.

___ Underline two details that set the mood.

◀ **Sample Text Markings**

Passage 7: The Orphan Train

1 A; *Sample answer:* I picked A because the second paragraph says that Hannah was an orphan. Then it says 'a child like her without parents'.

2 D; *Sample answer:* I think Hannah was worried because she was taking a long trip by herself across the country and didn't know anything about Kansas or farming or if she and her new family would like each other.

3 *Sample answer:* I think a prairie is flat, empty land that goes on and on.

4 *Sample answer:* The author says Hannah thought the prairie seemed like a lonely place. Besides being worried about her new life, I think she felt lonely, too. And she had been travelling alone on a train for days, so that would be lonely, as well.

Picnic for Three

Read the holiday story.
Then follow the instructions in the Text-Marking box.

Sasha, her dog, Petey, and her older cousin Mikel were in a rowing boat one August afternoon. Mikel was rowing them to a nearby island for a picnic. It was a short boat ride away. A light breeze blew and the sun was shining. The waves lapped gently against the boat.

Suddenly, the sun disappeared behind dark clouds and everything changed. The gentle breeze became a wild wind that blew Sasha's hair and whipped at her clothes. The water became choppy and rocked the small boat from side to side. Then it began to pour.

"We must get back to shore," Mikel yelled. He rowed as hard as he could to reach safety. Petey barked and shook, so Sasha held him close. With her free hand, she gripped her seat tightly. The picnic would have to wait.

Text Marking

Think about the setting and mood of the story.

☐ Draw a box around WHEN the story takes place.

◯ Circle WHERE the story takes place.

___ Underline three details that set the mood.

◀ **Sample Text Markings**

Passage 8: Picnic for Three

1 B; *Sample answer:* I picked B because the story says, 'one August afternoon'.

2 D; *Sample answer:* I picked D because at first it's a really nice sunny day and they're going to have a fun picnic. But when the weather gets stormy, the mood gets dangerous and a bit scary.

3 *Sample answer:* I think it means that they could feel the waves gently bumping into the boat.

4 *Sample answer:* The sudden storm meant that they couldn't keep rowing to the island for the picnic. It was more important to get back to shore safely.

Answers

Passage 9: Rusty Stones

9 Key Events & Details   Name _____   Date _____

Rusty Stones

Read the science-fiction story.
Then follow the instructions in the Text-Marking box.

Willa couldn't believe her eyes. There was a giant hole on her farm. Only the night before, tall corn had grown there. "What happened?" wondered Willa. She got off her tractor to explore the hole. Willa walked all the way around it. She saw packed dirt and rust-coloured blobs of stone.

Slowly, Willa stepped into the strange hole to grab a small stone. How heavy and warm it felt! Suddenly, the stone began to jiggle in her hand. A squeaky voice cried, "KLEEP!" Willa looked more closely. She saw a crack that was bright purple inside. She noticed that the other rusty stones had the same look. They were also jiggling.

"What?" Willa thought. "Did a fleet of tiny spaceships crash into my farm?"

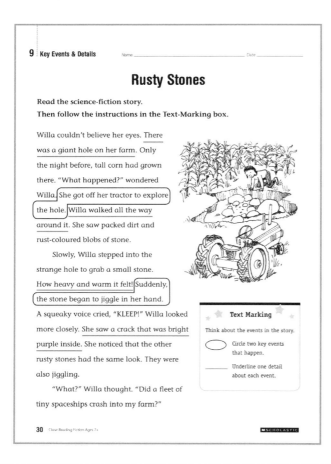

> **Text Marking**
> Think about the events in the story.
> ⬭ Circle two key events that happen.
> ___ Underline one detail about each event.

30 Close Reading Fiction Ages 7+   ■SCHOLASTIC

1 B; *Sample answer:* I picked B because that's what it said in the second paragraph.

2 A; *Sample answer:* I picked A because in the last sentence of the story, it says that's what Willa thought.

3 *Sample answer:* I think it shows the beginning, when Willa got off her tractor and went to look at the big hole.

4 *Sample answer:* It might mean "Help" or be a warning like, "Stay away!"

Passage 10: Where's Frankie?

10 Key Events & Details   Name _____   Date _____

Where's Frankie?

Read the mystery story.
Then follow the instructions in the Text-Marking box.

A funny thing happened one day when Ike went to feed Frankie. He was not in his tank or near it. Where had Ike's frog disappeared to?

Ike put down the frog food to search for his missing pet. He looked in the kitchen and behind the sofa in the living room. He searched under the beds in the bedrooms. He even opened all the cupboard doors and peeked in. No luck. Frankie was missing, and Ike was in tears.

"Now, THINK," Ike told himself, "What do frogs like? Where might Frankie want to be?" The lightbulb in Ike's head lit up brightly. He raced to the bathroom with a happy and knowing smile. There was Frankie in the bath by the plughole. He seemed to be smiling, too.

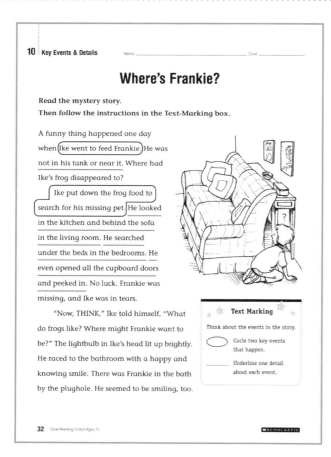

> **Text Marking**
> Think about the events in the story.
> ⬭ Circle two key events that happen.
> ___ Underline one detail about each event.

32 Close Reading Fiction Ages 7+   ■SCHOLASTIC

1 C; *Sample answer:* I picked C because Ike was upset that he couldn't find Frankie.

2 B; *Sample answer:* I picked B because Ike used his brain to think about where Ike might be. A bright lightbulb is like a bright idea.

3 *Sample answer:* Ike tried to think about where a frog would want to be. Frogs like water, so Ike checked the bathroom.

4 *Sample answer:* Ike's frog Frankie wasn't in his tank. Ike looked all over for him. He finally found Frankie in the bathtub.

Seeing the Seaport

Read the travel story.
Then follow the instructions in the Text-Marking box.

The Loh family entered the visitor centre of the old seaport. There they planned their day. They picked out which activities, displays and shows to see. They took a map of the seaport and began their tour.

First, the Lohs strolled all around the seaport. It looked as it did when it was filled with sailors, ship builders and workers. Guides dressed the way people did 150 years ago. They told sailing stories. They sang sea songs. They worked on their crafts as visitors watched.

Next, the Lohs boarded three old sailing ships. Macey especially liked the wooden whale boat. Devin liked the old-fashioned fire boat. Mr Loh said that visiting old ships can turn *landlubbers* into *sea dogs*.

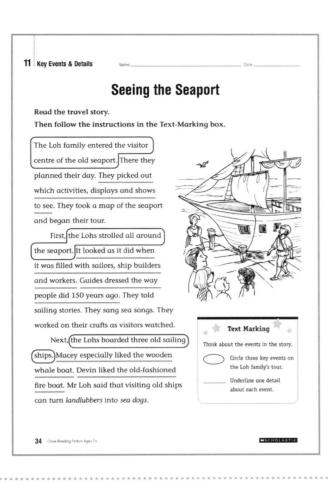

Text Marking

Think about the events in the story.

⬭ Circle three key events on the Loh family's tour.

____ Underline one detail about each event.

◀ **Sample Text Markings**

Passage 11: Seeing the Seaport

1 D; *Sample answer:* I picked D because that's the only thing that happened at the visitor centre.

2 B; *Sample answer:* I picked B because it sounds like 'land lovers'. Also, if a visit to a seaport can turn landlubbers into sea dogs then a landlubber probably is not someone who likes the sea to begin with.

3 *Sample answer:* I see how big and fancy an old whaling ship was, and can imagine how different that old ship looks compared to modern ships.

4 *Sample answer:* I think he meant that people might want to go sailing after learning so much at the old seaport.

A New Sitter

Read the realistic fiction story.
Then follow the instructions in the Text-Marking box.

① Roxy rang the doorbell at 6pm. She was the new babysitter. Tia frowned when Dad introduced them. "Where's Pam?" Tia grumbled. Pam was her usual sitter. Tia slumped onto the sofa. She folded her arms across her chest and began to sulk.

After Tia's dad left, Roxy knew just what to do. She suggested making puppets together. Tia's frown turned into a smile. Tia and Roxy made ② paper-bag puppets. They used them to put on a silly play. The girls laughed and giggled all evening.

③ Tia's dad returned just before bedtime. "Dad, can Roxy be my sitter next time?" Tia asked. "She's the best!"

Text Marking

Find the sequence of events for Tia's evening.

▭ Draw boxes around the signal words:
at 6pm, after and **before bedtime.**

____ Underline three important events.

1–2–3 Number the events in order.

◀ **Sample Text Markings**

Passage 12: A New Sitter

1 B; *Sample answer:* I picked B because I worked that out from the first paragraph.

2 C; *Sample answer:* I picked C because that's what happened between the beginning and the end.

3 *Sample answer:* Tia didn't expect to like Roxy, but Roxy came up with a fun project, and they had a good time together.

4 *Sample answer:* Give them a chance. Get to know them before you judge them.

Answers

Friends Play Putt-Putt

Read the sports story.
Then follow the instructions in the Text-Marking box.

(1) Mum took Kai and Emily to Putt-Putt to play mini-golf. The ⬚first⬚ thing they did was to choose their golf equipment. Each picked a putter and a ball. Emily chose a yellow ball and Kai took a blue one.

(2) ⬚Next,⬚ they walked to the golf course and looked it over.

(3) ⬚Then,⬚ Emily and Kai played the first hole. It was called Windmill. Kai went first and hit the ball with his putter. The ball hit the moving windmill and bounced back to him. Both children laughed. Kai's second putt was better. He and Emily both got their balls into the hole in five goes. Emily kept track of their scores.

(4) ⬚After⬚ they finished playing Windmill, the friends walked to the second hole. It was called Bridge. Emily went first this time. She aimed carefully at the narrow bridge...

Text Marking

Find the sequence of events at Putt-Putt.

⬚   Draw boxes around the signal words: **first**, **next**, **then** and **after**.

___   Underline the most important events.

1-2-3-4   Number the events in order.

◄ **Sample Text Markings**

Passage 13: Friends Play Putt-Putt

1 C; *Sample answer:* In the first paragraph, it says they each picked a putter. The other things are parts of the mini-golf course.

2 A; *Sample answer:* In paragraph 3, it says that both children got their balls in the hole after five goes.

3 *Sample answer:* They chose their putter and ball first, then they went to the course and looked it over.

4 Accept reasonable responses. *Sample answer:* The ball might hit the bridge and bounce back. But if Emily aims well, it might go over the bridge and end up near the hole.

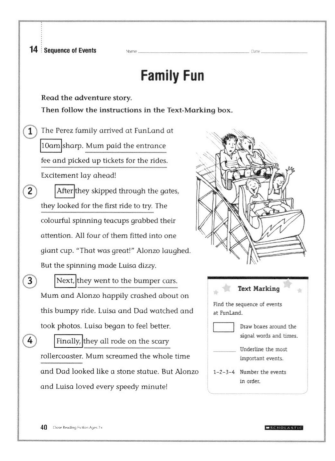

Family Fun

Read the adventure story.
Then follow the instructions in the Text-Marking box.

(1) The Perez family arrived at FunLand at ⬚10am⬚ sharp. Mum paid the entrance fee and picked up tickets for the rides. Excitement lay ahead!

(2) ⬚After⬚ they skipped through the gates, they looked for the first ride to try. The colourful spinning teacups grabbed their attention. All four of them fitted into one giant cup. "That was great!" Alonzo laughed. But the spinning made Luisa dizzy.

(3) ⬚Next,⬚ they went to the bumper cars. Mum and Alonzo happily crashed about on this bumpy ride. Luisa and Dad watched and took photos. Luisa began to feel better.

(4) ⬚Finally,⬚ they all rode on the scary rollercoaster. Mum screamed the whole time and Dad looked like a stone statue. But Alonzo and Luisa loved every speedy minute!

Text Marking

Find the sequence of events at FunLand.

⬚   Draw boxes around the signal words and times.

___   Underline the most important events.

1-2-3-4   Number the events in order.

◄ **Sample Text Markings**

Passage 14: Family Fun

1 A; *Sample answer:* I picked A because I counted the rides. First they did the teacups, next they did the bumper cars, then the rollercoaster.

2 D; *Sample answer:* I picked D because Luisa got dizzy on the first ride and probably wanted to wait until she felt better.

3 *Sample answer:* They skipped through the gates which showed that they were happy and eager to get to the rides.

4 *Sample answer:* Alonzo and Luisa loved it, but Mum and Dad were nervous and scared.

■SCHOLASTIC

Fishing for the Moon

Read the Chinese folktale.
Then follow the instructions in the Text-Marking box.

One clear night, Quan went to fetch water. He got a big surprise when he reached the village well. Deep down in the water was the moon. Its silvery face looked up at Quan.

"What a problem! Poor moon is stuck!" cried Quan as he raced home for his largest hook. He tied it to his bucket. Back at the well, he lowered the bucket to fish out the moon.

He jiggled the hook until he felt it catch. How he pulled and tugged! He yanked so hard that the rope on the bucket broke. Quan fell flat on his back. But when he looked up, the moon was back up high in the sky! Quan puffed up with pride. His plan had worked. He was the hero who rescued the moon.

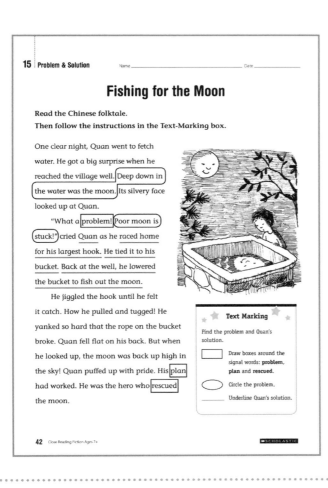

Text Marking

Find the problem and Quan's solution.

☐ Draw boxes around the signal words: **problem**, **plan** and **rescued**.

◯ Circle the problem.

___ Underline Quan's solution.

◀ **Sample Text Markings**

Passage 15: Fishing for the Moon

1 D; *Sample answer:* I picked D because the story says this in the first paragraph.

2 A; *Sample answer:* I picked A because Quan thought he had saved the moon from being stuck in the well.

3 *Sample answer:* He needed water from the well there.

4 *Sample answer:* No, I don't think Quan was a hero. He believed the moon was really in the well, but it was just a reflection. The moon was in the sky all along, but Quan didn't notice it. So he really didn't rescue anything.

Bear Tale

Read the tall tale.
Then follow the instructions in the Text-Marking box.

Uncle Jake likes to tell a tale of trouble he found while exploring a cave in the woods. The problem was that he surprised a bear named Grizz. Grizz stood up tall and let out a mighty roar.

The first thought Uncle Jake had was to run. He ran as fast as he could. But Grizz ran after him and was catching up. Then Uncle Jake had a clever idea – he dropped his camera. That stopped Grizz in his tracks. Grizz grabbed the camera, took a selfie and rolled over laughing.

Grizz called Uncle Jake over to show him the photo. Uncle Jake laughed, too. That's how man and bear became friends. Whenever Uncle Jake is in those woods, he finds Grizz. They take pictures until they fall down giggling.

Text Marking

Find the problem and the solutions.

☐ Draw boxes around the signal words: **trouble**, **problem**, **first thought** and **clever idea**.

◯ Circle the problem.

___ Underline two solutions.

◀ **Sample Text Markings**

Passage 16: Bear Tale

1 B; *Sample answer:* I picked B because the story says this in the first paragraph.

2 A; *Sample answer:* I picked A because the story says that in paragraph 2.

3 *Sample answer:* He couldn't run fast or far enough to get away from Grizz. So he had to think of something else, and FAST!

4 *Sample answer:* Bears don't know how to use cameras or take selfies, they don't laugh and they don't make friends with people.

Answers

17 Context Clues   Name _____   Date _____

Ozzie's Goal

Read the circus story.
Then follow the instructions in the Text-Marking box.

Ozzie's dad performed in the circus. He did tricks on the high wire. He danced, walked backwards and spun around up there and made it look easy! Ozzie (admired) his dad; he was his hero. But Ozzie didn't want to be exactly like him.

Ozzie's dream was to juggle. (He set his heart on it.) Dee-Dee the Clown helped by giving him beanbags to work with. Beanbags don't break or roll away when they drop. Dee-Dee used them to learn juggling herself. It was hard for Ozzie at first. But he practised every day. Ozzie wanted to learn to juggle very much.

After a month, Ozzie was juggling beanbags easily. "Soon you'll be juggling eggs!" Dee-Dee said with a wink. That did it – Ozzie had his next goal. He would get good enough to juggle raw eggs!

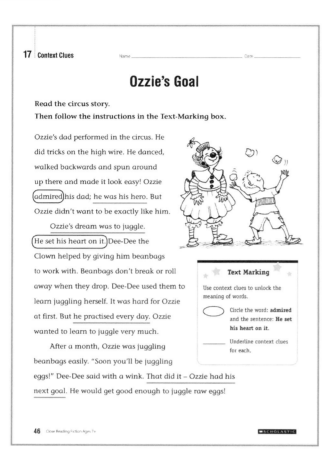

Text Marking

Use context clues to unlock the meaning of words.

- ⬭ Circle the word: **admired** and the sentence: **He set his heart on it.**
- ___ Underline context clues for each.

46 Close Reading Fiction Ages 7+   **SCHOLASTIC**

◀ **Sample Text Markings**

Passage 17: Ozzie's Goal

1 B; *Sample answer:* I picked B because Ozzie's dad is his hero, so he looks up to him.

2 C; *Sample answer:* I picked C because juggling is hard, so if you want to learn it, you must practise.

3 *Sample answer:* When you set your heart on something, you really want it. You work hard to make it happen. In the story, Ozzie set his heart on learning to juggle. That's what he wanted. That was his goal.

4 *Sample answer:* Dee-Dee knew that eggs break if you drop them and jugglers do drop things as they learn. Ozzie is getting better, but has a way to go before he can juggle raw eggs.

---

18 Context Clues   Name _____   Date _____

Holding Hands

Read the family story.
Then follow the instructions in the Text-Marking box.

Ellie, Dad and her little brother Luke drove to the shopping centre. Twelve-year-old Ellie sat in the back seat, safely wearing her seatbelt. But Luke was just two years old. He was tucked into his car seat beside her. Ellie kept turning her head around like an owl. She played 'Peek-a-Boo' with Luke to hear his happy giggle.

After getting out of the car, Dad (clutched) Luke's right hand. The three walked towards the shopping centre together. Luke's tiny hand disappeared into Dad's (immense) one. Ellie knew that Luke felt protected. Ellie remembered that secure feeling herself. She also used to hold her father's huge hand when she was learning to walk. She always knew Dad would keep her safe. She knew that Luke would be safe, too.

Text Marking

Use context clues to unlock the meanings of words.

- ⬭ Circle the words: **clutched** and **immense**.
- ___ Underline context clues for each word.

48 Close Reading Fiction Ages 7+   **SCHOLASTIC**

◀ **Sample Text Markings**

Passage 18: Holding Hands

1 D; *Sample answer:* I picked D because the picture shows the dad holding little Luke's hand. Also, near the end of the story I read that Ellie used to hold her father's hand, too.

2 B; *Sample answer:* I picked B because the story says this in the second paragraph.

3 *Sample answer:* Ellie likes making Luke laugh, which shows that she cares about him. She also understands how important it is to keep him safe.

4 *Sample answer:* 'Immense' means big. The picture shows a little child's hand beside a large adult's hand.

19 Compare & Contrast Name ______ Date ______

A Pair of Pots

Read the art story.
Then follow the instructions in the Text-Marking box.

Lamar loved working with clay. He took a pottery class. The last class was a pottery party. The students took turns describing two different pots they made. Lamar talked about his coil pot and his slab pot.

"For both pots, I used red clay that dries hard," said Lamar. "I used only my hands to make the coil pot. First I made a long clay snake. Then I coiled it around and around into a pot. I smoothed the inside to finish it.

"But for the slab pot, I used tools and my hands. I used a rolling pin to flatten the clay. I used a knife to cut five squares. I pieced them together into a pot. Then I smoothed all the seams."

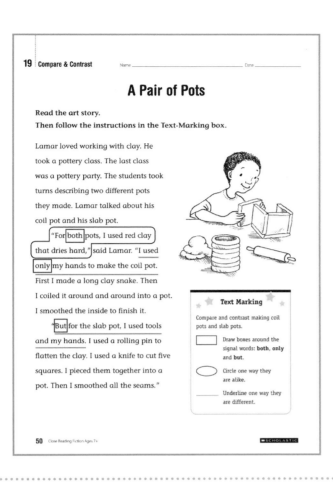

Text Marking

Compare and contrast making coil pots and slab pots.

- Draw boxes around the signal words: **both**, **only** and **but**.
- Circle one way they are alike.
- Underline one way they are different.

50 Close Reading Fiction Ages 7+ SCHOLASTIC

Sample Text Markings

Passage 19: A Pair of Pots

1 C; *Sample answer:* I picked C because it is the only statement that is true.

2 A; *Sample answer:* I picked A because Lamar said that in his talk.

3 *Sample answer:* For a coil pot, you use your hands to make a long snake of clay and wind it around into a pot shape. For a slab pot, you use tools to flatten and then cut the clay into large flat pieces that you put together to form a pot.

4 *Sample answer:* The boy is working on the slab pot, putting flat pieces together. But it also shows a round coil pot, with the coiled outside.

20 Compare & Contrast Name ______ Date ______

Spring Play

Read the theatre story.
Then follow the instructions in the Text-Marking box.

Nikki, Meg and Hari took part in the spring play at Pine Forest School. It was a musical set in a kingdom from long ago. Meg and Hari acted in the play. But Nikki took part in a different way. She was the director. She helped the actors do their best. Nikki told them where to stand, how to speak and sing, and how to move around the stage.

Meg starred as the king. She got to wear a shiny gold crown and a long purple robe. By contrast, Hari played a jester. He wore a pointy hat with bells. Nikki taught him a funny dance, which he learned quickly and well.

The play was a hit. The whole audience cheered at the end, so Meg, Hari, Nikki and the others took five bows!

Text Marking

Compare and contrast what Nikki, Meg and Hari did in the story.

- Draw boxes around the signal words: **but**, **different** and **by contrast**.
- Circle two things they did that was the same.
- Underline things they did that were different.

52 Close Reading Fiction Ages 7+ SCHOLASTIC

Sample Text Markings

Passage 20: Spring Play

1 B; *Sample answer:* I picked B because in the first paragraph it says that Nikki helped the actors do their best.

2 D; *Sample answer:* I picked D because Hari was the jester who did a funny dance.

3 *Sample answer:* It says in the last paragraph that everyone cheered and the actors took five bows, so I think it means that people really liked it a lot.

4 *Sample answer:* Both children acted in the play. But Meg was the king. Hari was a jester. He also did a funny dance.

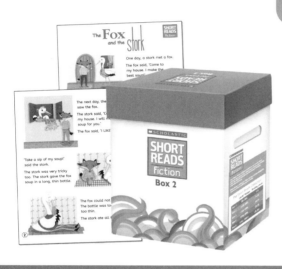